The Mediterranean Diet Cookbook

Easy and Delicious Recipes to Burns Fat

and Lose Weight Fast

YVONNE TILLERY

© Copyright 2021 By Yvonne Tillery - All rights reserved.

The content contained within this book may not be reproduced, duplicated or transmitted without direct written permission from the author or the publisher. Under no circumstances will any blame or legal responsibility be held against the publisher, or author, for any damages, reparation, or monetary loss due to the information contained within this book. Either directly or indirectly.

Legal Notice:

This book is copyright protected. This book is only for personal use. You cannot amend, distribute, sell, use, quote or paraphrase any part, or the content within this book, without the consent of the author or publisher.

Disclaimer Notice:

Please note the information contained within this document is for educational and entertainment purposes only. All effort has been executed to present accurate, up to date, and reliable, complete information. No warranties of any kind are declared or implied. Readers acknowledge that the author is not engaging in the rendering of legal, financial, medical or professional advice. The content within this book has been derived from various sources. Please consult a licensed professional before attempting any techniques outlined in this book.

By reading this document, the reader agrees that under no circumstances is the author responsible for any losses, direct or indirect, which are incurred as a result of the use of information contained within this document, including, but not limited to, errors, omissions, or inaccuracies

Table Of Contents

BREAKFAST RECIPES 7
    1.   BAKED EGGS & SAUSAGE MUFFINS 8
    2.   VEGGIE STUFFED HASH BROWNS 10
    3.   CRUSTLESS SUN-DRIED TOMATO QUICHE 13
    4.   ARTICHOKE FRITTATA 15
    5.   SPINACH CURRY PANCAKES WITH APPLE, RAISINS, AND CHICKPEAS 18

LUNCH 21
    6.   TARRAGON COD FILLETS 22
    7.   SALMON AND RADISH MIX 24
    8.   SMOKED SALMON AND WATERCRESS SALAD 26
    9.   SALMON AND CORN SALAD 28
    10. COD AND MUSHROOMS MIX 30

DINNER 32
    11. MEDITERRANEAN PEARL COUSCOUS 33
    12. ITALIAN STYLE GROUND BEEF 36
    13. FLAVORFUL BEEF BOURGUIGNON 38
    14. CAULIFLOWER TOMATO BEEF 40
    15. DINNER PARTY BRISKET 42

SIDE DISHES 45

16.	Beans and Rice	46
17.	Artichoke alla Romana	48
18.	Balsamic Asparagus	51
19.	Lime Cucumber Mix	53
20.	Walnuts Cucumber Mix	55

VEGETABLES 56

21.	Crispy Zucchini Fritters	57
22.	Cheesy Spinach Pies	59
23.	Instant Pot Black Eyed Peas	61
24.	Green Beans and Potatoes in Olive Oil	63
25.	Nutritious Vegan Cabbage	65

APPETIZERS AND SNACKS 67

26.	Zucchini-Ricotta Fritters with Lemon-Garlic Aioli	68
27.	Salmon-Stuffed Cucumbers	71
28.	Sfougato	73
29.	Goat Cheese–Mackerel Pâté	75
30.	Baba Ghanoush	77

PASTA 79

31.	Chicken Spinach and Artichoke Stuffed Spaghetti Squash 80	
32.	Angel Hair with Asparagus-Kale Pesto	83
33.	Spicy Pasta Puttanesca	85

34.	Roasted Vegetarian Lasagna	87
35.	Artichoke Chicken Pasta	90

SALADS 92

36.	Olives and Lentils Salad	93
37.	Lime Spinach and Chickpeas Salad	95
38.	Minty Olives and Tomatoes Salad	96
39.	Beans and Cucumber Salad	97
40.	Tomato and Avocado Salad	99

Breakfast Recipes

1. Baked Eggs & Sausage Muffins

Preparation Time:

Cooking Time: 20 minutes

Servings: 2

Ingredients:

- 3 eggs
- ¼ cup cream
- 2 sausages, boiled
- Chopped fresh herbs
- Sea salt to taste
- 4 tablespoons cheese, grated
- 1 piece of bread, sliced lengthwise

Directions:

1. Preheat your air fryer to 360°Fahrenheit. Break the eggs in a bowl, add cream, and scramble. Grease 3 muffin cups with cooking spray.
2. Add equal amounts of egg mixture into each. Arrange sliced sausages and bread slices into muffin cups, sinking into egg mixture.
3. Sprinkle the tops with cheese, and salt to taste. Cook the muffins for 20-minutes. Season with fresh herbs and serve warm.

Nutrition: Calories: 242, Total Fat: 12.5, Carbs: 10.2g, Protein: 14.3g

2. Veggie Stuffed Hash Browns

Preparation Time: 10 minutes

Cooking Time: 20 minutes

Servings: 4

Ingredients:

- Olive oil cooking spray
- 1 tablespoon plus 2 teaspoons olive oil, divided
- 4 ounces (113 g) baby bella mushrooms, diced
- 1 scallion, white parts and green parts, diced
- 1 garlic clove, minced
- 2 cups shredded potatoes
- 1/2 teaspoon salt
- 1/4 teaspoon black pepper
- 1 Roma tomato, diced

- 1/2 cup shredded Mozzarella

Directions:

1. Preheat the air fryer to 380ºF (193ºC). Lightly coat the inside of a 6-inch cake pan with olive oil cooking spray.
2. In a small skillet, heat 2 teaspoons olive oil over medium heat. Add the mushrooms, scallion, and garlic, and cook for 4 to 5 minutes, or until they have softened and are beginning to show some color. Remove from heat.
3. Meanwhile, in a large bowl, combine the potatoes, salt, pepper, and the remaining tablespoon olive oil. Toss until all potatoes are well coated.
4. Pour half of the potatoes into the bottom of the cake pan. Top with the mushroom mixture, tomato, and Mozzarella. Spread the remaining potatoes over the top.
5. Bake in the air fryer for 12 to 15 minutes, or until the top is golden brown.
6. Remove from the air fryer and allow to cool for 5 minutes before slicing and serving.

Nutrition: calories: 164 fat: 9g protein: 6g carbs: 16g fiber: 3g sodium: 403mg

3. Crustless Sun-Dried Tomato Quiche

Preparation Time: 15 minutes

Cooking Time: 25 minutes

Servings: 4

Ingredients:

- 6 large eggs
- ¼ cup goat cheese
- 2 tablespoons milk
- Pinch cayenne pepper
- 1 teaspoon extra-virgin olive oil
- 2 shallots, finely chopped
- ½ teaspoon minced garlic
- 10 sun-dried tomatoes, quartered
- 1 teaspoon chopped fresh parsley
- Pinch sea salt

- Pinch freshly ground black pepper

Directions:

1. Preheat the oven to 375°F.
2. In a medium bowl, whisk the eggs, goat cheese, milk, and cayenne pepper to blend.
3. Place a 9-inch ovenproof skillet over medium-high heat and add the olive oil.
4. Add the shallots and garlic to the skillet, and sauté for about 2 minutes until tender.
5. Pour in the egg mixture. Scatter the sun-dried tomatoes and parsley evenly over the top.
6. Season the quiche with sea salt and pepper.
7. Cook the quiche, lifting the edges to allow the uncooked egg to flow underneath, for about 3 minutes until the bottom is firm.
8. Place the skillet in the oven and bake for about 20 minutes until the egg is cooked through, golden, and puffy.
9. Cooking tip: If you have leftover quiche, wrap it in a tortilla the next day for an easy, hearty lunch or breakfast.

Nutrition: Calories: 171 Total Fat: 11g Saturated Fat: 4 Carbohydrates: 5g Fiber: 1g Protein: 13g

4. Artichoke Frittata

Preparation Time: 5 minutes

Cooking Time: 10 minutes

Servings: 4

Ingredients:

- 8 large eggs
- ¼ cup grated Asiago cheese
- 1 tablespoon chopped fresh basil
- 1 teaspoon chopped fresh oregano
- Pinch sea salt
- Pinch freshly ground black pepper
- 1 teaspoon extra-virgin olive oil
- 1 teaspoon minced garlic

- 1 cup canned, water-packed, quartered artichoke hearts, drained
- 1 tomato, chopped

Directions:

1. Preheat the oven to broil.
2. In a medium bowl, whisk the eggs, Asiago cheese, basil, oregano, sea salt, and pepper to blend.
3. Place a large ovenproof skillet over medium-high heat and add the olive oil. Add the garlic and sauté for 1 minute.
4. Remove the skillet from the heat and pour in the egg mixture.
5. Return the skillet to the heat and evenly sprinkle the artichoke hearts and tomato over the eggs.
6. Cook the frittata without stirring for about 8 minutes, or until the center is set.
7. Place the skillet under the broiler for about 1 minute, or until the top is lightly browned and puffed.
8. Cut the frittata into 4 pieces and serve.
9. Substitution tip: If you don't need a vegetarian dish, add chopped cooked chicken, cooked shrimp, or smoked salmon to this frittata for extra protein.

Nutrition: Calories 199 Total Fat: 13g Saturated Fat: 5g Carbohydrates: 5g Fiber: 2g Protein: 16g

5. Spinach Curry Pancakes with Apple, Raisins, And Chickpeas

Preparation Time: 20 minutes

Cooking Time: 40 minutes

Servings: 6

Ingredients:

- 2 lg eggs
- 1/3 C finely chopped fresh cilantro
- 1/4 tsp. black pepper
- 2 1/2 C 1% milk
- 1 C plus 2 tbsp all-purpose flour
- 1 yellow onion, chopped
- 1 can (15.5 oz) chickpeas, rinsed and drained

- 1 granny smith apple, diced
- 1/4 C golden raisins
- 2 tbsp. madras curry powder
- 10 oz. fresh spinach
- lemon wedges, for serving

Directions:

1. In a blender, puree eggs, cilantro, pepper, 1 cup of milk and flour, 2- tablespoons of oil, and 1/4 teaspoon of salt. Lightly brush the 10 "non-stick skillet with cooking spray and heat over medium heat. Pour 1/3 cup of batter evenly into pan and cook until edges set, 1 minute. Flip and cook for 30 seconds. Repeat for remaining pancakes. Cover to keep warm.
2. Heat the remaining 1- tablespoon of oil in a skillet over medium heat. Add onion and keep cooking until soften, 5-minutes. Add chickpeas, apple, raisins, and curry powder—Cook for 3 minutes. Stir in the remaining 2- tablespoons of flour through and cook for 30 seconds. Stir in the remaining 1-1/2 cup milk. Cook until thick, 2 minutes. Add spinach and the remaining 1/2 teaspoon of salt.

Nutrition: 106 calories, 5.04 g pro, 14.66 g carbohydrates, 2.4 g fiber, 4.08 g sugars 3.27 g fat 80 mg Chol, 85mg sodium

Lunch

6. Tarragon Cod Fillets

Preparation Time: 10 minutes

Cooking Time: 12 minutes

Servings: 4

Ingredients:

- 4 cod fillets, boneless
- ¼ cup capers, drained
- 1 tablespoon tarragon, chopped
- Sea salt and black pepper to the taste
- 2 tablespoons olive oil
- 2 tablespoons parsley, chopped
- 1 tablespoon olive oil
- 1 tablespoon lemon juice

Directions:

1. Heat up a pan with the oil over medium-high heat, add the fish and cook for 3 minutes on each side.
2. Add the rest of the ingredients, cook everything for 7 minutes more, divide between plates and serve.

Nutrition: calories 162, fat 9.6, fiber 4.3, carbs 12.4, protein 16.5

7. Salmon and Radish Mix

Preparation Time: 10 minutes

Cooking Time: 15 minutes

Servings: 4

Ingredients:

- 2 tablespoons olive oil
- 1 tablespoon balsamic vinegar
- 1 and ½ cup chicken stock
- 4 salmon fillets, boneless
- 2 garlic cloves, minced
- 1 tablespoon ginger, grated
- 1 cup radishes, grated
- ¼ cup scallions, chopped

Directions:

1. Heat up a pan with the oil over medium-high heat, add the salmon, cook for 4 minutes on each side and divide between plates
2. Add the vinegar and the rest of the ingredients to the pan, toss gently, cook for 10 minutes, add over the salmon and serve.

Nutrition: calories 274, fat 14.5, fiber 3.5, carbs 8.5, protein 22.3

8. Smoked Salmon and Watercress Salad

Preparation Time: 5 minutes

Cooking Time: 0 minutes

Servings: 4

Ingredients:

- 2 bunches watercress
- 1-pound smoked salmon, skinless, boneless and flaked
- 2 teaspoons mustard
- ¼ cup lemon juice
- ½ cup Greek yogurt
- Salt and black pepper to the taste
- 1 big cucumber, sliced
- 2 tablespoons chives, chopped

Directions:

1. In a salad bowl, combine the salmon with the watercress and the rest of the ingredients toss and serve right away.

Nutrition: calories 244, fat 16.7, fiber 4.5, carbs 22.5, protein 15.6

9. Salmon and Corn Salad

Preparation Time: 5 minutes

Cooking Time: 0 minutes

Servings: 4

Ingredients:

- ½ cup pecans, chopped
- 2 cups baby arugula
- 1 cup corn
- ¼ pound smoked salmon, skinless, boneless and cut into small chunks
- 2 tablespoons olive oil
- 2 tablespoon lemon juice
- Sea salt and black pepper to the taste

Directions:

1. In a salad bowl, combine the salmon with the corn and the rest of the ingredients, toss and serve right away.

Nutrition: calories 284, fat 18.4, fiber 5.4, carbs 22.6, protein 17.4

10.   Cod and Mushrooms Mix

Preparation Time: 10 minutes

Cooking Time: 25 minutes

Servings: 4

Ingredients:

- 2 cod fillets, boneless
- 4 tablespoons olive oil
- 4 ounces mushrooms, sliced
- Sea salt and black pepper to the taste
- 12 cherry tomatoes, halved
- 8 ounces lettuce leaves, torn
- 1 avocado, pitted, peeled and cubed
- 1 red chili pepper, chopped
- 1 tablespoon cilantro, chopped
- 2 tablespoons balsamic vinegar
- 1-ounce feta cheese, crumbled

Directions:

1. Put the fish in a roasting pan, brush it with 2 tablespoons oil, sprinkle salt and pepper all over and broil under medium-high heat for 15 minutes. Meanwhile, heat up a pan with the rest of the oil over medium heat, add the mushrooms, stir and sauté for 5 minutes.
2. Add the rest of the ingredients, toss, cook for 5 minutes more and divide between plates.
3. Top with the fish and serve right away.

Nutrition: calories 257, fat 10, fiber 3.1, carbs 24.3, protein 19.4

Dinner

11. Mediterranean Pearl Couscous

Preparation Time: 4 minutes

Cooking Time: 10 minutes

Servings: 6

Ingredients:

For the Lemon Dill Vinaigrette:

- 1 large lemon, juice of
- 1/3 cup Extra virgin olive oil
- 1 tsp dill weed
- 1 tsp garlic powder
- Salt and pepper

For the Israeli Couscous:

- 2 cups Pearl Couscous, Israeli Couscous
- Extra virgin olive oil

- 2 cups grape tomatoes, halved
- 1/3 cup finely chopped red onions
- 1/2 English cucumber
- 15 oz. can chickpeas
- 14 oz. can good quality artichoke hearts
- 1/2 cup Kalamata olives
- 15–20 fresh basil leaves
- 3 oz. fresh baby mozzarella or feta cheese

Directions:

1. Make the lemon-dill vinaigrette, scourge lemon juice, olive oil, dill weed, garlic powder, salt and pepper then keep aside
2. In a medium-sized heavy pot, heat two tbsp. of olive oil
3. Sauté the couscous in the olive oil briefly until golden brown, then add cups of boiling water (or follow the instructed on the package), and cook according to package.
4. Once done, drain in a colander, set aside in a bowl and allow to cool
5. In a large mixing bowl, combine the extra virgin olive oil, grape tomatoes, red onions, cucumber, chickpeas, artichoke hearts, and Kalamata olives

6. Then add in the couscous and the basil, mix together gently
7. Now, give the lemon-dill vinaigrette a quick whisk and add to the couscous salad, mix to combine
8. Taste and adjust salt, if needed
9. Distribute among the containers, store for 2-3 days
10. To Serve: Add in the mozzarella cheese, garnish with more fresh basil and enjoy!

Nutrition: Calories: 393 Fat: 13g Protein: 13g

12. Italian Style Ground Beef

Preparation Time: 10 minutes

Cooking Time: 20 minutes

Servings: 4

Ingredients:

- 2 lbs. ground beef
- 2 eggs, lightly beaten
- 1/4 tsp dried basil
- 3 tbsp olive oil
- 1/2 tsp dried sage
- 1 1/2 tsp dried parsley
- 1 tsp oregano
- 2 tsp thyme
- 1 tsp rosemary
- Pepper
- Salt

Directions:

1. Pour 1 1/2 cups of water into the instant pot then place the trivet in the pool.
2. Spray loaf pan with cooking spray.

3. Add all ingredients into the mixing bowl and mix until well combined.
4. Transfer meat mixture into the prepared loaf pan and place loaf pan on top of the trivet in the pot.
5. Seal pot with lid and cook on high for 35 minutes.
6. Once done, allow to release pressure naturally for 10 minutes then release remaining using quick release. Remove lid.
7. Serve and enjoy.

Nutrition: Calories 365 Fat 18 g Carbohydrates 0.7 g Sugar 0.1 g Protein 47.8 g Cholesterol 190 mg

13.   Flavorful Beef Bourguignon

Preparation Time: 10 minutes

Cooking Time: 20 minutes

Servings: 4

Ingredients:

- 1 1/2 lbs. beef chuck roast, cut into chunks
- 2/3 cup beef stock
- 2 tbsp fresh thyme
- 1 bay leaf
- 1 tsp garlic, minced
- 8 oz mushrooms, sliced
- 2 tbsp tomato paste
- 2/3 cup dry red wine
- 1 onion, sliced
- 4 carrots, cut into chunks

- 1 tbsp olive oil
- Pepper
- Salt

Directions:

1. Add oil into the instant pot and set the pot on sauté mode.
2. Add meat and sauté until brown. Add onion and sauté until softened.
3. Add remaining ingredient and stir well.
4. Seal pot with lid and cook on high for 12 minutes.
5. Once done, allow to release pressure naturally. Remove lid.
6. Stir well and serve.

Nutrition: Calories 744 Fat 51.3 g Carbohydrates 14.5 g Sugar 6.5 g Protein 48.1 g Cholesterol 175 mg

14. Cauliflower Tomato Beef

Preparation Time: 10 minutes

Cooking Time: 25 minutes

Servings: 2

Ingredients:

- 1/2 lb beef stew meat, chopped
- 1 tsp paprika
- 1 celery stalk, chopped
- 1 tbsp balsamic vinegar
- 1/4 cup grape tomatoes, chopped
- 1 onion, chopped
- 1/4 cup cauliflower, chopped
- 1 tbsp olive oil
- Pepper
- Salt

Directions:

1. Add oil into the instant pot and set the pot on sauté mode.
2. Add meat and sauté for 5 minutes.
3. Add remaining ingredients and stir well.
4. Seal pot with lid and cook on high for 20 minutes.
5. Once done, allow to release pressure naturally. Remove lid.
6. Stir and serve.

Nutrition: Calories 306 Fat 14.3 g Carbohydrates 7.6 g Sugar 3.5 g Protein 35.7 g Cholesterol 101 mg

15.   Dinner Party Brisket

Preparation Time: 15 minutes

Cooking Time: 11 hours 5 minutes

Servings: 8

Ingredients:

- 1 fresh beef brisket, trimmed
- 3 tsp. dried Italian seasoning, crushed and divided
- 1 can diced tomatoes with basil, garlic and oregano with juice
- 1/2 C. olives, pitted
- 1 tsp. lemon peel, grated finely
- Pinch salt and freshly ground black pepper, to taste
- 1/2 C. low-sodium beef broth
- 2 medium fennel bulbs, trimmed, cored and cut into wedges
- 2 tbsp. all-purpose flour

- 1/4 C. cold water

Directions:

1. Season the brisket with 1 tsp. of the Italian seasoning.
2. In a bowl, add the remaining Italian seasoning, tomatoes with juice, olives, lemon peel, salt, black pepper and broth and mix well.
3. In a slow cooker, place the brisket and top with fennel, followed by the tomato mixture.
4. Set the slow cooker on "Low" and cook, covered for about 10-11 hours.
5. Uncover the slow cooker and with a slotted spoon, transfer the brisket and vegetables onto a platter.
6. With a piece of foil, cover the meat to keep warm.
7. Skim off the fat from the top of cooking liquid.
8. In a small pan, add about 2 C. of the cooking liquid over medium heat.
9. In a small bowl, dissolve the flour in water.
10. In the pan of cooking liquid, add the flour mixture, stirring continuously.
11. Cook for about 2-3 minutes or until desired thickness of sauce, stirring continuously.

12. Cut the brisket into desired sized slices and serve with the topping of gravy.

Nutrition: Calories: 367; Carbohydrates: 8.g; Protein: 53.3g; Fat: 12.3g; Sugar: 1.5g; Sodium: 266mg; Fiber: 2.8g

Side Dishes

16. Beans and Rice

Preparation Time: 10 minutes

Cooking Time: 55 minutes

Servings: 6

Ingredients:

- 1 tablespoon olive oil
- 1 yellow onion, chopped
- 2 celery stalks, chopped
- 2 garlic cloves, minced
- 2 cups brown rice
- 1 and ½ cup canned black beans, rinsed and drained
- 4 cups water
- Salt and black pepper to the taste

Directions:

1. Heat up a pan with the oil over medium heat, add the celery, garlic and the onion, stir and cook for 10 minutes. Add the rest of the ingredients, stir, bring to a simmer and cook over medium heat for 45 minutes. Divide between plates and serve.

Nutrition: 224 calories 8.4g fat 3.4g fiber 15.3g carbs 6.2g protein

17. Artichoke alla Romana

Preparation Time: 10 minutes

Cooking Time: 50 minutes

Servings: 3

Ingredients:

- 3 artichokes (ideal would be the "Mammole" variety),
- 1 bunch of mint
- 1 clove of garlic
- Salt to taste
- Black pepper to taste
- 7 tablespoons of extra virgin olive oil
- 1 lemon

Directions:

1. Start by cutting the lemon in half. Then fill a rather large bowl with water and squeeze half a lemon inside.
2. Take your artichokes and start removing the outer leaves by tearing them with your hands. Then cut the end of the stem and the tip of the artichoke. Once again, with your hands, spread the artichoke, and using a small knife cut into the central part in order to eliminate the inner beard.
3. Peel away the stem as well and round the end using a sharp knife. Place the artichoke in the water from step 1 and repeat this process for the others. Cover the bowl with paper towels which will keep the artichokes immersed in the water, set aside and take care of the filling in the meantime.
4. Take the mint and mince it. Switch to the garlic, peel it and chop it as well, adding it to the mint along with a pinch of salt and black pepper. Mix everything.

5. Drain the artichokes and beat them lightly to remove excess water, then use the mixture prepared in step 4 to stuff them. Season with salt and pepper and transfer them into a pan upside down, keeping them rather close together. Then pour in both the oil and the water: the artichokes must be covered up to the beginning of their stems.
6. Cover with a lid and cook for about 30 minutes on low heat. After that, you can serve your warm artichokes alla Romana!

<u>Nutrition</u>: 515 Calories 8g Carbs 5.1g Protein 10.4g Fiber

18.   Balsamic Asparagus

Preparation Time: 10 minutes

Cooking Time: 15 minutes

Servings: 4

Ingredients:

- 3 tablespoons olive oil
- 3 garlic cloves, minced
- 2 tablespoons shallot, chopped
- Salt and black pepper to the taste
- 2 teaspoons balsamic vinegar
- 1 and ½ pound asparagus, trimmed

Directions:

1. Heat up a pan with the oil over medium-high heat, add the garlic and the shallot and sauté for 3 minutes.

Add the rest of the ingredients, cook for 12 minutes more, divide between plates and serve as a side dish.

Nutrition: 100 calories 10.5g fat 1.2g fiber 2.3g carbs 2.1g protein

19.   Lime Cucumber Mix

Preparation Time: 10 minutes

Cooking Time: 0 minute

Servings: 8

Ingredients:

- 4 cucumbers, chopped
- ½ cup green bell pepper, chopped
- 1 yellow onion, chopped
- 1 chili pepper, chopped
- 1 garlic clove, minced
- 1 teaspoon parsley, chopped
- 2 tablespoons lime juice
- 1 tablespoon dill, chopped
- Salt and black pepper to the taste
- 1 tablespoon olive oil

Directions:

1. In a large bowl, mix the cucumber with the bell peppers and the rest of the ingredients, toss and serve as a side dish.

Nutrition: 123 calories 4.3g fat 2.3g fiber 5.6g carbs 2g protein

20.   Walnuts Cucumber Mix

Preparation Time: 5 minutes

Cooking Time: 0 minute

Servings: 2

Ingredients:

- 2 cucumbers, chopped
- 1 tablespoon olive oil
- Salt and black pepper to the taste
- 1 red chili pepper, dried
- 1 tablespoon lemon juice
- 3 tablespoons walnuts, chopped
- 1 tablespoon balsamic vinegar
- 1 teaspoon chives, chopped

Directions:

1. In a bowl, mix the cucumbers with the oil and the rest of the ingredients, toss and serve as a side dish.

Nutrition: 121 calories 2.3g fat 2g fiber 6.7g carbs 2.4g protein

Vegetables

21.   Crispy Zucchini Fritters

Preparation Time: 15 minutes

Cooking Time: 20 minutes

Servings: 6

Ingredients:

- 2 large green zucchinis
- 1 cup flour
- 1 large egg, beaten
- ½ cup water
- 1 teaspoon baking powder

Directions:

1. Grate the zucchini into a large bowl.

2. Add the 2 tbsp. of parsley, 3 garlic cloves, salt, flour, egg, water, and baking powder to the bowl and stir to combine.
3. In a large pot or fryer over medium heat, heat oil to 365°F.
4. Drop the fritter batter into 3 cups of vegetable oil. Turn the fritters over using a slotted spoon and fry until they are golden brown, about 2 to 3 minutes.
5. Strain fritters from the oil and place on a plate lined with paper towels.
6. Serve warm with Creamy Tzatziki or Creamy Traditional Hummus as a dip.

<u>Nutrition</u>: 446 Calories 5g Protein 19g Carbohydrates

22. Cheesy Spinach Pies

Preparation Time: 20 minutes

Cooking Time: 40 minutes

Servings: 5

Ingredients:

- 2 tablespoons extra-virgin olive oil
- 3 (1-pound) bags of baby spinach, washed
- 1 cup feta cheese
- 1 large egg, beaten
- Puff pastry sheets

Directions:

1. Preheat the oven to 375°F.
2. Using big skillet over medium heat, cook the olive oil, 1 onion, and 2 garlic cloves for 3 minutes.
3. Add the spinach to the skillet one bag at a time, letting it wilt in between each bag. Toss using tongs. Cook for 4 minutes. Once cooked, strain any extra liquid from the pan.
4. Mix feta cheese, egg, and cooked spinach.

5. Lay the puff pastry flat on a counter. Cut the pastry into 3-inch squares.
6. Place a tablespoon of the spinach mixture in the center of a puff-pastry square. Turn over one corner of the square to the diagonal corner, forming a triangle. Crimp the edges of the pie by pressing down with the tines of a fork to seal them together. Repeat until all squares are filled.
7. Situate the pies on a parchment-lined baking sheet and bake for 25 to 30 minutes or until golden brown. Serve warm or at room temperature.

<u>Nutrition</u>: 503 Calories 16g Protein 38g Carbohydrates

23. Instant Pot Black Eyed Peas

Preparation Time: 6 minutes

Cooking Time: 25 minutes

Servings: 4

Ingredients:

- 2 cups black-eyed peas (dried)
- 1 cup parsley, dill
- 2 slices oranges
- 2 tbsp. tomato paste
- 4 green onions
- 2 carrots, bay leaves

Directions:

1. Clean the dill thoroughly with water removing stones.
2. Add all the ingredients in the instant pot and stir well to combine.
3. Lid the instant pot and set the vent to sealing.
4. Set time for twenty-five minutes. When the time has elapsed release pressure naturally.
5. Serve and enjoy the black-eyed peas.

Nutrition: 506 Calories 14g Protein 33g Carbohydrates

24. Green Beans and Potatoes in Olive Oil

Preparation Time: 12 minutes

Cooking Time: 17 minutes

Servings: 4

Ingredients:

- 15 oz. tomatoes (diced)
- 2 potatoes
- 1 lb. green beans (fresh)
- 1 bunch dill, parsley, zucchini
- 1 tbsp. dried oregano

Directions:

1. Turn on the sauté function on your instant pot.
2. Pour tomatoes, a cup of water and olive oil. Stir in the rest of the ingredients and stir through.

3. Close the instant pot and click the valve to seal. Set time for fifteen minutes.
4. When the time has elapsed release pressure. Remove the Fasolakia from the instant pot. Serve and enjoy.

Nutrition: 510 Calories 20g Protein 28g Carbohydrates

25.   Nutritious Vegan Cabbage

Preparation Time: 35 minutes

Cooking Time: 15 minutes

Servings: 6

Ingredients:

- 3 cups green cabbage
- 1 can tomatoes, onion
- Cups vegetable broth
- 3 stalks celery, carrots
- 2 tbsp. vinegar, sage

Directions:

1. Mix 1 tbsp. of lemon juice. 2 garlic cloves and the rest of ingredients in the instant pot and. Lid and set time for fifteen minutes on high pressure.

2. Release pressure naturally then remove the lid. Remove the soup from the instant pot.
3. Serve and enjoy.

<u>Nutrition:</u> 67 Calories 0.4g Fat 3.8g Fiber

Appetizers and Snacks

26. Zucchini-Ricotta Fritters with Lemon-Garlic Aioli

Preparation Time: 30 minutes

Cooking Time: 25 minutes

Servings: 4

Ingredients:

- 1 large zucchini
- 1 teaspoon salt, divided
- ½ cup whole-milk ricotta cheese
- 2 scallions
- 1 large egg
- 2 garlic cloves
- 2 tablespoons fresh mint (optional)
- 2 teaspoons grated lemon zest
- ¼ teaspoon freshly ground black pepper
- ½ cup almond flour

- 1 teaspoon baking powder
- 8 tablespoons extra-virgin olive oil
- 8 tablespoons Roasted Garlic Aioli

Directions:

1. Place the shredded zucchini in a colander or on several layers of paper towels. Sprinkle with ½ teaspoon salt and let sit for 10 minutes. Using another layer of paper towel, press down on the zucchini to release any excess moisture and pat dry.
2. In a large bowl, combine the drained zucchini, ricotta, scallions, egg, garlic, mint (if using), lemon zest, remaining ½ teaspoon salt, and pepper and stir well.
3. Blend almond flour and baking powder. Mix in flour mixture into the zucchini mixture and let rest for 10 minutes.
4. In a large skillet, working in four batches, fry the fritters. For each batch of four, heat 2 tablespoons olive oil over medium-high heat. Add 1 heaping tablespoon of zucchini batter per fritter, pressing down with the back of a spoon to form 2- to 3-inch fritters. Cover and let fry 2 minutes before flipping. Fry another 2 to 3 minutes, covered.

5. Repeat for the remaining three batches, using 2 tablespoons of the olive oil for each batch.
6. Serve with aioli.

<u>Nutrition</u>: 448 Calories 42g Fat 8g Protein 8g Carbohydrates

27.   Salmon-Stuffed Cucumbers

Preparation Time: 10 minutes

Cooking Time: 0 minute

Servings: 4

Size/ Portion: 1 piece

Ingredients:

- 2 large cucumbers, peeled
- 1 (4-ounce) can red salmon
- 1 medium very ripe avocado
- 1 tablespoon extra-virgin olive oil
- Zest and juice of 1 lime
- 3 tablespoons chopped fresh cilantro
- ½ teaspoon salt
- ¼ teaspoon black pepper

Directions:

1. Slice the cucumber into 1-inch-thick segments and using a spoon, scrape seeds out of center of each segment and stand up on a plate.
2. In a medium bowl, mix salmon, avocado, olive oil, lime zest and juice, cilantro, salt, and pepper.

3. Spoon the salmon mixture into the center of each cucumber segment and serve chilled.

Nutrition: 159 Calories 11g Fat 9g Protein 20g Carbohydrates

28.   Sfougato

Preparation Time: 9 minutes

Cooking Time: 13 minutes

Servings: 4

Size/ Portion: 2 tablespoons

Ingredients:

- ½ cup crumbled feta cheese
- ¼ cup bread crumbs
- 1 medium onion
- 4 tablespoons all-purpose flour
- 2 tablespoons fresh mint
- ½ teaspoon salt
- ½ teaspoon ground black pepper
- 1 tablespoon dried thyme
- 6 large eggs, beaten
- 1 cup water

Directions:

1. In a medium bowl, mix cheese, bread crumbs, onion, flour, mint, salt, pepper, and thyme. Stir in eggs.
2. Spray an 8" round baking dish with nonstick cooking spray. Pour egg mixture into dish.

3. Place rack in the Instant Pot® and add water. Fold a long piece of foil in half lengthwise. Lay foil over rack to form a sling and top with dish. Cover loosely with foil. Seal lid, put steam release in Sealing, select Manual, and time to 8 minutes.
4. When the timer alarms, release the pressure. Uncover. Let stand 5 minutes, then remove dish from pot.

Nutrition: 274 Calories 14g Fat 17g Protein 13g Carbohydrates

29. Goat Cheese–Mackerel Pâté

Preparation Time: 10 minutes

Cooking Time: 0 minute

Servings: 4

Ingredients:

- 4 ounces olive oil-packed wild-caught mackerel
- 2 ounces goat cheese
- Zest and juice of 1 lemon
- 2 tablespoons chopped fresh parsley
- 2 tablespoons chopped fresh arugula
- 1 tablespoon extra-virgin olive oil
- 2 teaspoons chopped capers
- 2 teaspoons fresh horseradish (optional)

Directions:

1. In a food processor, blender, or large bowl with immersion blender, combine the mackerel, goat cheese, lemon zest and juice, parsley, arugula, olive oil, capers, and horseradish (if using). Process or blend until smooth and creamy.

2. Serve with crackers, cucumber rounds, endive spears, or celery.

Nutrition: 118 Calories 8g Fat 9g Protein 15g Carbohydrates

30. Baba Ghanoush

Preparation Time: 9 minutes

Cooking Time: 11 minutes

Servings: 8

Size/ Portion: 3 tablespoons

Ingredients:

- 2 tablespoons extra-virgin olive oil
- 1 large eggplant
- 3 cloves garlic
- ½ cup water
- 3 tablespoons fresh flat-leaf parsley
- ½ teaspoon salt
- ¼ teaspoon smoked paprika
- 2 tablespoons lemon juice

- 2 tablespoons tahini

Directions:

1. Press the Sauté button on the Instant Pot® and add 1 tablespoon oil. Add eggplant and cook until it begins to soften, about 5 minutes. Add garlic and cook 30 seconds.
2. Add water and close lid, click steam release to Sealing, select Manual, and time to 6 minutes. Once the timer rings, quick-release the pressure. Select Cancel and open lid.
3. Strain cooked eggplant and garlic and add to a food processor or blender along with parsley, salt, smoked paprika, lemon juice, and tahini. Add remaining 1 tablespoon oil and process. Serve warm or at room temperature.

Nutrition: 79 Calories 6g Fat 2g Protein 3g Carbohydrates

Pasta

31. Chicken Spinach and Artichoke Stuffed Spaghetti Squash

Preparation Time: 10 minutes.

Cooking Time: 23 minutes.

Servings: 4

Ingredients:

- 4 oz reduced-fat cream cheese, cubed and softened
- 1/4 tsp ground pepper
- 3 tbsp water
- 1/4 tsp salt
- Crushed red peppers
- 3 lb spaghetti squash, halved lengthwise and seeded
- 1/2 cup shredded parmesan cheese
- 5 oz pack baby spinach
- 10 oz pack artichoke hearts, chopped
- Diced fresh basil

Directions:

1. On a microwaveable dish, place your squash halves with the cut side facing up. Add 2 tbsp of water to the squash. Set the microwave to high and cook without covering the dish for about 15 minutes. You can also place the squash on a prepared baking sheet (rimmed) and bake at 400 degrees F for 40 minutes.
2. Set your stove to medium heat and place a large skillet containing 1 tbsp of water on it. Add spinach into the pan and stir while it cooks for about 5 minutes, or until the vegetable wilts. Drain the spinach and place in a bowl.
3. Place the rack in the upper third region of your oven, then preheat your broiler.
4. Using a fork, scrape squash from each shell half, and place them in a bowl. Add artichoke hearts, pepper, salt, cream cheese, and ¼ cup parmesan into the bowl of squash. Mix well. Place squash shells on a baking sheet, and add the squash mixture into the shells. Add the remaining parmesan on top and broil for 3 minutes.
5. Garnish with red pepper and basil, and serve.

Nutrition: Cal: 223, Protein: 10.2g, Carbohydrates: 23.3g, Fiber: 8.6g, Fat: 10.9g, Sat. Fat: 5.7g

32. Angel Hair with Asparagus-Kale Pesto

Preparation Time: 10 minutes

Cooking Time: 10 minutes

Servings: 6

Ingredients:

- ¾ pound asparagus, woody ends removed, and coarsely chopped
- ¼ pound kale, thoroughly washed
- ½ cup grated Asiago cheese
- ¼ cup fresh basil
- ¼ cup extra-virgin olive oil
- Juice of 1 lemon
- Sea salt
- Freshly ground black pepper
- 1-pound angel hair pasta
- Zest of 1 lemon

Directions:

1. In a food processor, pulse the asparagus and kale until very finely chopped.
2. Add the Asiago cheese, basil, olive oil, and lemon juice and pulse to form a smooth pesto.
3. Season with sea salt and pepper and set aside.
4. Cook the pasta al dente according to the package directions. Drain and transfer to a large bowl.
5. Add the pesto, tossing well to coat
6. Sprinkle with lemon zest and serve.
7. Cooking tip: You can make the asparagus pesto up to 3 days ahead. Keep it refrigerated until you need it.

Nutrition: Calories: 283; Total Fat: 12g; Saturated Fat: 2g; Carbohydrates: 33g; Fiber: 2g; Protein: 10g

33. Spicy Pasta Puttanesca

Preparation Time: 10 minutes

Cooking Time: 20 minutes

Servings: 4

Ingredients:

- 2 teaspoons extra-virgin olive oil
- ½ sweet onion, finely chopped
- 2 teaspoons minced garlic
- 1 (28-ounce) can sodium-free diced tomatoes
- ½ cup chopped anchovies
- 2 teaspoons chopped fresh oregano
- 2 teaspoons chopped fresh basil
- ½ teaspoon red pepper flakes
- ½ cup quartered Kalamata olives

- ¼ cup sodium-free chicken broth
- 1 tablespoon capers, drained and rinsed
- Juice of 1 lemon
- 4 cups cooked whole-grain penne

Directions:

1. In a large saucepan over medium heat, heat the olive oil.
2. Add the onion and garlic, and sauté for about 3 minutes until softened.
3. Stir in the tomatoes, anchovies, oregano, basil, and red pepper flakes. Bring the sauce to a boil and reduce the heat to low. Simmer for 15 minutes, stirring occasionally.
4. Stir in the olives, chicken broth, capers, and lemon juice.
5. Cook the pasta according to the package directions and serve topped with the sauce.
6. Ingredient tip: Do not mistake sardines for anchovies, although they are both small, silvery fish sold in cans. Anchovies are usually salted in brine and matured to create a distinctive, rich taste.

Nutrition: Calories: 303; Total Fat: 6g; Saturated Fat: 0g; Carbohydrates: 54g; Fiber: 9g; Protein: 9g

34. Roasted Vegetarian Lasagna

Preparation Time: 25 minutes

Cooking Time: 50 minutes

Servings: 6

Ingredients:

- 1 eggplant, thickly sliced
- 2 zucchini, sliced lengthwise
- 1 yellow squash, sliced lengthwise
- 1 sweet onion, thickly sliced
- 2 tablespoons extra-virgin olive oil
- 1 (28-ounce) can sodium-free diced tomatoes
- 1 cup quartered, canned, water-packed artichoke hearts, drained
- 2 teaspoons minced garlic
- 2 teaspoons chopped fresh basil
- 2 teaspoons chopped fresh oregano
- Pinch red pepper flakes
- 12 no-boil whole-grain lasagna noodles
- ¾ cup grated Asiago cheese

Directions:

1. Preheat the oven to 400°F.
2. Line a baking sheet with aluminum foil and set aside.
3. In a large bowl, toss together the eggplant, zucchini, yellow squash, onion, and olive oil to coat.
4. Arrange the vegetables on the prepared sheet and roast for about 20 minutes, or until tender and lightly caramelized.
5. Chop the roasted vegetables well and transfer them to a large bowl.
6. Stir in the tomatoes, artichoke hearts, garlic, basil, oregano, and red pepper flakes
7. Spoon one-quarter of the vegetable mixture into the bottom of a deep 9-by-13-inch baking dish.
8. Arrange 4 lasagna noodles over the sauce.
9. Repeat, alternating sauce and noodles, ending with sauce.
10. Sprinkle the Asiago cheese evenly over the top. Bake for about 30 minutes until bubbly and hot.
11. Remove from the oven and cool for 15 minutes before serving.

12. Substitution tip: If having a vegetarian meal is not a requirement, lean ground beef (92%) or ground chicken can be added to the roasted vegetable sauce for a more robust meal. Brown the ground meat in a skillet and add it to the finished sauce before assembling the lasagna.

Nutrition: Calories: 386; Total Fat: 11g; Saturated Fat: 3g; Carbohydrates: 59g; Fiber: 12g; Protein: 15g

35.   Artichoke Chicken Pasta

Preparation Time: 20 minutes

Cooking Time: 5 minutes

Servings: 4

Ingredients:

- 2 cloves garlic, crushed
- 2 lemons, wedged
- 2 tbsp. lemon juice
- 14 oz. artichoke hearts, chopped
- 1-lb. chicken breast fillet, diced
- ½ cup feta cheese, crumbled
- 1 tbsp. olive oil
- 16 oz. whole-wheat (gluten-free) pasta of your choice
- 3 tbsp. parsley, chopped
- ½ cup red onion, chopped
- 2 tsp. oregano
- 1 tomato, chopped
- Ground black pepper and salt, to taste

Directions:

1. Pour the water into a deep saucepan and boil it. Add the pasta and some salt; cook it as per package directions. Drain the water and set aside the pasta.
2. Over medium stove flame, heat the oil in a skillet or saucepan (preferably of medium size).
3. Sauté the onions and garlic until softened and translucent, stir in between.
4. Add the chicken and cook until it is no longer pink.
5. Mix in the tomatoes, artichoke hearts, parsley, feta cheese, oregano, lemon juice and the cooked pasta.
6. Combine well and cook for 3-4 minutes, stirring frequently.
7. Season with black pepper and salt. Garnish with lemon wedges and serve warm.

Nutrition: Calories – 486|Fat – 10g|Carbs – 42g|Fiber – 9g|Protein – 37g

Salads

36.   Olives and Lentils Salad

Preparation Time: 10 minutes

Cooking Time: 0 minutes

Servings: 2

Ingredients:

- 1/3 cup canned green lentils
- 1 tablespoon olive oil
- 2 cups baby spinach
- 1 cup black olives
- 2 tablespoons sunflower seeds
- 1 tablespoon Dijon mustard
- 2 tablespoons balsamic vinegar
- 2 tablespoons olive oil

Directions:

1. Mix the lentils with the spinach, olives, and the rest of the ingredients in a salad bowl, toss and serve cold.

Nutrition: 279 Calories 6.5g Fat 12g Protein

37.   Lime Spinach and Chickpeas Salad

Preparation Time: 10 minutes

Cooking Time: 0 minutes

Servings: 4

Ingredients:

- 16 ounces canned chickpeas
- 2 cups baby spinach leaves
- ½ tablespoon lime juice
- 2 tablespoons olive oil
- 1 teaspoon cumin, ground
- ½ teaspoon chili flakes

Directions:

1. Mix the chickpeas with the spinach and the rest of the ingredients in a large bowl, toss and serve cold.

Nutrition: 240 Calories 8.2g Fat 12g protein

38. Minty Olives and Tomatoes Salad

Preparation Time: 10 minutes

Cooking Time: 0 minutes

Servings: 4

Ingredients:

- 1 cup kalamata olives
- 1 cup black olives
- 1 cup cherry tomatoes
- 4 tomatoes
- 1 red onion, chopped
- 2 tablespoons oregano, chopped
- 1 tablespoon mint, chopped
- 2 tablespoons balsamic vinegar
- ¼ cup olive oil
- 2 teaspoons Italian herbs, dried

Directions:

1. In a salad bowl, mix the olives with the tomatoes and the rest of the ingredients, toss, and serve cold.

Nutrition: 190 Calories 8.1g Fat 4.6g Protein

39. Beans and Cucumber Salad

Preparation Time: 10 minutes

Cooking Time: 0 minutes

Servings: 4

Ingredients:

- 15 oz canned great northern beans
- 2 tablespoons olive oil
- ½ cup baby arugula
- 1 cup cucumber
- 1 tablespoon parsley
- 2 tomatoes, cubed
- 2 tablespoon balsamic vinegar

Directions:

1. Mix the beans with the cucumber and the rest of the ingredients in a large bowl, toss and serve cold.

Nutrition: 233 Calories 9g Fat 8g protein

40. Tomato and Avocado Salad

Preparation Time: 10 minutes

Cooking Time: 0 minutes

Servings: 4

Ingredients:

- 1-pound cherry tomatoes
- 2 avocados
- 1 sweet onion, chopped
- 2 tablespoons lemon juice
- 1 and ½ tablespoons olive oil
- Handful basil, chopped

Directions:

1. Mix the tomatoes with the avocados and the rest of the ingredients in a serving bowl, toss and serve right away.

Nutrition: 148 Calories 7.8g Fat 5.5g Protein

www.ingramcontent.com/pod-product-compliance
Lightning Source LLC
Chambersburg PA
CBHW070940080526
44589CB00013B/1593